Keys to Becoming God's Phenomenal Woman!

Your journey to

new levels of success begins...........

By Dr. Lorelle Strong Rich

On Purpose Publications, Nashville, TN

Keys to Becoming God's Phenomenal Woman!

Published by
On Purpose Publications
Nashville, TN
www.onpurposepublications.com
Copyright © 2012

ISBN 978-0-9827061-5-2

Cover design by Vincent Alexander and PrecisionFX Graphics

Printed in the United States of America

ENDORSEMENTS

"Dr. Rich gives relevance to the ageless truths and principles found in the Scriptures and empowers every woman to break the bonds of her worldly limitations and stand strong in the light of who she is in God. Dr. Rich also guides a woman to look inside herself and toward the Lord, she helps women find the power they need to unlock their destiny and excel."

--**Bishop Joseph W. Walker III, D. Min., Senior Pastor Mt. Zion Baptist Church, Nashville, TN.**

"Dr. Lorelle Rich's book on becoming a phenomenal woman is phenomenal. Read it, absorb it, apply its lessons and you will enrich your life emotionally and spiritually."

--**Attorney David Hudson, First Amendment Center & Vanderbilt University**

"Phenomenal things happen to your life and the lives of those around you when you activate the principles Dr. Rich shares in her latest book. <u>Keys to Becoming God's Phenomenal Woman</u> allows women to see more of their true potential and power in God. It's a must read!"

--**Erin M. Anderson, mother and educator**

DEDICATION

I would like to dedicate this book to my greatest friend, the Holy Spirit. You are my comforter, guide and counselor. You have been the essence of my womanhood and guide of my fingers through the writing of this book.

I would also like to dedicate this book to my phenomenal mother, Pastor Cynthia Strong, and brother, John Strong, for years of encouragement. And to my loving husband Senior Pastor, Michael Rich and my children, Majesty and Michael Jr. for your unending love and prayers.

Keys to Becoming God's Phenomenal Woman!

Table of Contents

Introduction: God is Still Thinking About You..................... 1

My Personal Journey... 9

Expect Phenomenal Breakthroughs 17

Maintain Discipline in Challenging Times 29

Now is the Time to Move Beyond the Ordinary 35

Activation for Phenomenal Breakthroughs 41

Raise Up Your Expectations 45

The Importance of Starving the Flesh to Obtain God's Best
.... 53

Are You Ready For Spiritual Battle.................................. 59

The Wrestling Match 67

How to deal with a Seemingly Dead Situation................... 73

Keys to Tapping into Your Unlimited Faith....................... 83

What is the Root of Our Actions 91

Never Give Up!... 101

Your Present Condition is Not Your Permanent Condition
.... 105

Aim for Victory 109

On the Verge of a Breakthrough..................................... 113

Keys to Opening the Doors of Blessings ....
.... 117

Conclusion/Reflection Time.. 127

INTRODUCTION

God is Still Thinking about You

As you walk the steps of destiny there are

times you will come across milestones that force you

to PUSH even harder! I believe this is a season that

God wants to show Himself in a phenomenal way.

The word "phenomenal" means something

extraordinary, unusual, and supernatural. You must

believe if you are reading this book it is not by

coincidence. This is your Divine season to step into

a NEW door of God's anointing to cause a supernatural change turnaround in your life. As a woman of God you must understand that there are keys to walk in Phenomenal Breakthroughs! Yet with the power of God residing within you, the victory is already WON! You must have a made up your mind to overcome and not allow the distractions of the enemy or your flesh to detour you from your destiny! You must allow your faith to paralyze the hand of the enemy and stand in the Kingdom , despite what you might be seeing in the natural. You are called to BREAKTHROUGH natural circumstances because of the "greater one" within you! You must refuse to settle for less than God's Best and stir forth your phenomenal faith within and decree that YOUR season of supernatural

manifestations has ARRIVED!

I am speaking to women of God who must

recognize that God wants them to transition out of

the ordinary and into the extraordinary. You cannot

settle for where you are. Phenomenal is when the

power of God is resting in the inside of you. You

have the faith to stand and do all you can do to

continue to stand. To be a **phenomenal woman**

means *to take a chance, be a risk-taker, to make*

God first in an extraordinary way. A description of

a phenomenal woman of God is displayed in the

Word of God, which says: *"A capable, intelligent,*

and virtuous woman-who can find her? She is far

*more precious than jewels and her value is far above rubies or pearls (*Proverbs 31:10AMP)." The description of this woman puts her in a category of extraordinary, not just because of her natural achievements alone, but also her heart's desire to keep God first in her heart and destiny.

Therefore, the incredible determination to push through natural circumstances is the formulation of a phenomenal woman. The value of this woman outweighs natural jewels and the uniqueness of this woman is not easily found, yet she does exist and a piece of this phenomenal description lies in each of us. The key is making the choice and standing with an attitude that refuses to be defeated despite the obstacles that we all must

face in life. The Word says: " *Little children, you*
are of God [you belong to Him] and have [already]
defeated and overcome them [the agents of the
antichrist], because He Who lives in you is greater
*(mightier) than he who is in the world." (*1 John
4:4AMP). The power of God inside of you is
relative to the intimacy of God. I challenge you to
ask yourself: Do you really know Him?

> *Take [with me] your share of the hardships*
> *and suffering [which you are called to*
> *endure] as a good (first-class) soldier of*
> *Christ Jesus. No soldier when in service gets*
> *entangled in the enterprises of [civilian] life;*
> *his aim is to satisfy and please the one who*
> *enlisted him. And if anyone enters competitive*

*games, he is not crowned unless he competes lawfully (fairly, according to the rules laid down). [It is] the hard-working farmer [who labors to produce] who must be the first partaker of the fruits. (*2 Timothy 2:3-6 AMP)

Woman of God you must believe that your destiny is worth the Fight. . You do not have to fight with words, but fight in the spiritual realm. You must put on the Godly armor, including the helmet of salvation, to keep your mind in a sober place. If not, the enemy will ensnare you. You must apply your full armor and one very important element is your helmet of salvation. Itt serves as your protection. When you put on the Helmet of salvation, your radar should go off when there's something trying to come up that is ungodly and evil. You have to stir forth the dynamic power of God in the inside of you, if you are to put a stop to the effect of negative words. . Thus, you must realize when other people's announcements about you are greater than God's pronouncement; you need to have your own proclamation. Every now and then you have to make some pronouncement about your life. As soon as you do announce some things, be ready to fight. Be able to stand on what you pronounce over your life through the Word of God!

As women of God we are constantly being challenged by God to take "Phenomenal" steps in our destiny. I love that God does not base His choice on our past, but according to His Divine will for our lives. As you lay hold to new doors of opportunity, it is imperative that you are equipped with the proper keys that will ensure great results. As I reflect on my own destiny, I must take a moment to share some areas God used to shape me and my destiny in a phenomenal way!

MY PERSONAL JOURNEY

As the journey of my ministry began, I did

not realize that I was about to embrace a

phenomenal journey that would be life changing,

not just for myself, but for others whose lives I

would touch. I am a witness that God will divinely

interrupt your life and cause a "Phenomenal Shift"

without asking your permission. This sort of

reminds me of Esther in the Bible who was just an

ordinary girl with an extraordinary destiny. I am

sure, nowhere in the innermost parts of her mind could she have ever dreamed of becoming a queen. God already knew the phenomenal journey of her destiny and would challenge her to be a crusader to bring transformation for her people in the midst of possibly losing her OWN LIFE. Now, that is Phenomenal! (**Read the Book of Esther**)

Similar to Esther, God put me on a crusader's journey when He allowed me to become the "FIRST" woman in the history of a historic Baptist church in Nashville, Tennessee, to be ordained. Now please keep in mind Nashville, Tenn., is known as the "Bible Belt." In other words, it has some rigid religious thinking. Yet God chose this young, unique, radical young lady just graduating from

Vanderbilt University's Divinity School to be the

one He chose to BREAKTHROUGH the doors for

women in the ministry. Please let me be back up for

a moment. I was like Esther minding my own

business. I was always a believer, but just a typical

person going to church. I was a young lady who

had her dreams on television and the law. I attended

Howard University to study television production.

Once I completed my undergraduate degree, I

planned to study Law and become an entertainment

lawyer. Yet, like Esther, the Mordecia in my life,

the Holy Spirit kept agitating me. . In the midst of

my time at Howard University, I had an encounter

with the Holy Spirit when He came in my room one

day and I began to speak in tongues supernaturally

while crying my eyes out over a relationship (smile…those boyfriend relationships). I even called my mom when this occurred and she encouraged me to just allow God to have His way and trust the process!

As time moved forward, I read the book **"Good Morning Holy Spirit"** by Benny Hinn and it changed my life! It was during my time at Howard that I would go to the lower level of the library and spend hours just with the Holy Spirit. Amazingly, I was so hungry for Him that I would have amazing encounters. I would spend intimate times in prayer and worship. This is how I learned to really know the Holy Spirit and how He moves in the Spiritual realm. I believe this intimate time also released His scepter of favor upon my life, as it did

Esther in the Bible. You will see when you read the

rest of the story.

Now let's jump forward to my senior year at

Howard University. I was ready to become a

lawyer. I told God if He wanted me to preach the

Gospel, that He would have to do something

PHONOMENAL. Now what I did not share is

during the summer going into my senior year I had a

phenomenal dream. In this bright light, people

followed me and the Holy Spirit told me to minister

the Gospel. Now please keep in mind I was still

doing my THING!! So, I am a witness that God

calls you anytime. Now, I was always a LADY with

CLASS and STANDARDS...thank goodness, but I

still needed more of God!

So like Esther, God graduated me in the Kingdom and showed Himself in a phenomenal way by having Vanderbilt Divinity School send me an acceptance letter saying I was APPROVED with a partial scholarship. Now, let me be clear I DID NOT apply to Vanderbilt at all. I was applying to law schools that were on the east coast, not Divinity schools, and let me add I absolutely sent NO paper work to Vanderbilt Divinity School. I DID NOT take a graduate test to get in like the rest of my colleagues, nor did I go through an interview process. (AMAZING!!!) So like Esther in the Bible, God took my life and supernaturally stepped in. I had no other choice than to submit to His will.

Now you see why I believe as women we are phenomenal because of journeys God takes us on. Yet to stay on these journeys we must have phenomenal ingredients working within us. I mean to be the first woman to be ordained in a historical Baptist church was NO easy task. I had to be willing to press through some barriers and take risks. I did this to make it easier for other women to walk down a similar path. I must say I thank God for a loving mother and a brother who always made me feel like number one. I also thank God for my Bishop, who took the risk to ordain me. I choose to believe my leader must have seen something of diligence and perseverance to even choose me for the task that changed history at my church and my life.

Now I am proud to say due to my STAND there have been numerous women who have walked through the doors of that church that birthed me forth all because I chose to take that phenomenal journey! I bless God for the Mordecia in my life, also known as the Holy Spirit. Without my relationship with HIM (Holy Spirit) I would have not made it through the journey! Please women of God get to know Him as a person, not just as a feeling or a dove, but as a counselor, a guide, an encourager, a truth seeker and MORE!! He is REAL!! **(Read the Book of John)**

EXPECT A PHENOMENAL BREAKTHROUGH

These are some elements of the birthing forth of a

phenomenal woman:

- Phenomenal women are women who work

  tirelessly, personally, professionally,

  spiritually and socially to make this world a

  better place.

- Phenomenal women have a heart's desire to

  keep God first in their lives, families, and

  endeavors.

- Phenomenal women have spiritual discernment. They have the ability to accurately understand the timing of God for their lives. They realize that everything has a process. There will always be things the enemy tries to intimidate, but he does not dominant.

- Phenomenal women come to be a part of the vision of a church. The anointing on their lives sets the atmosphere. The aroma of their praise is pleasing to God, even though areas of their souls are going through the matrix.

- Phenomenal women determine to keep trivial things from interrupting their destiny. They operate in the principle of the law of association. In other words they know when to leave a situation. They understand they can't stay in situations too long or get into illegal covenants with things that cause a detour from their covenant with God.

- Phenomenal women are warfare people, not welfare people. If you're on welfare, it should be temporary. You can't get too comfortable with anything that will cause you to settle for less.

- Phenomenal women know how to operate their money, and know the seasons of sowing. You're always going through different stages, as your soul (will, mind, and intellect) is being renewed.

- Phenomenal women are flexible and they refuse to settle for mediocrity. They are women of integrity who hold strong to the Word of God and trust in God's ability, instead of their own.

- Phenomenal women are breaking through religion and tapping into the fullness of the Gospel of Jesus Christ! The application of intercession, praying in the Spirit, prophecy, casting out devils, healing and worship are a part of their daily lifestyle!

You may ask yourself if you have these ingredients. The answer is Yes! Please understand the step of change that we walk through as women of God is something every phenomenal woman must walk through. In this type of process you must allow carnality to be cut while you work through the process of CHANGE! As this occurs ensure that you gauge your thinking. You will get entangled with unnecessary weights. Some fail to gauge their thinking. Most women are overwhelmed because they maximize the problem, instead of the promises of God. They have made the problem phenomenal, not God. Phenomenal women don't just hear the Word; they apply it and make the WORD bigger than the situation!

Woman of God as you grab hold to your new confidence of purpose and destiny you must know this is a season that God is maturing you in the area of disciplining your flesh. The flesh is a taker. Your flesh is selfish and manipulative. When you know that at any moment you could slip into carnality, it should keep you in a place of humility. Humbleness will protect you from the enemy. There's strength in humility and serving. The enemy can't find you because you are low in humility. Please keep in mind humility is in your heart. Ask God to create in you a clean heart, in order, to ensure the process of transformation continues towards your phenomenal change internally and externally.

As you march forward to the triumphant beat of God, we as Kingdom women must stay in position to receive Kingdom orders from the Spirit realm on a daily basis. In order, for us to continue to mature forth in being phenomenal women we must understand the protocol of getting results.

I believe this book will help you as a woman to birth forth Phenomenal Kingdom results in your life, relationships, family and ministry!

As you begin to read this book, start now applying these keys for PHENOMENAL results in your life:

1) Spend time getting to know the Holy Spirit as a friend and daily apply the Word of God.

2) When you sense your identity getting low, fill up with worship, prayer and praise.

3) Allow the Spirit of faith to rise up in your inner person with daily confessions of the Word of God.

4) You must keep praise playing in your ears. No longer be passive this season. Get free by taking your inheritance by force.

5) Apply more tenacity this season. You are not wrestling with flesh and blood. Since the enemy is going to keep his assignment to kill, steal and destroy, be persistent and diligent to keep your assignment in the kingdom.

TIME FOR REFLECTION:

1) Remember it is your season to take your destiny by force; therefore, you have to be around some people that know how to get their inheritance back. You have to be around people that are mountain movers. List some people in your life who are mountain movers and then list some who are mountain blockers in your life.

_____

_____

_____

_____

_____

_____

_____

_____

_____

_____

_____

_____

2) Now what steps are you going to take to

cause a change?

_____

_____

_____

_____

_____

_____

_____

_____

_____

_____

_____

_____

3) You must find what keeps your momentum in God. What things in your life activate your faith to move forward? What area is God challenging you to break forth?

_____

_____

_____

_____

_____

_____

_____

_____

_____

_____

_____

_____

_____

_____

_____

_____

_____

MAINTAIN DISCIPLINE IN CHALLENGING TIMES

In various times of my life I have had to examine my emotions to ensure I remained in a faith posture to ward off the arrows of the Enemy as a Pastor and Prophet of God. Despite the office of ministry I walk in, I am still a woman that feels real pain and hurt. I am possibly speaking to a woman in ministry right now, and I want to encourage you to not let go of your dream. I have found one of the most challenging things in ministry is working with other women in the church. It is amazing that when you are a woman leader, the level of respect has to be earned at a double measure than for a man. In the midst of your press to earn respect you are constantly spending extra hours of support and love: wiping the tears from women's faces, praying them through repetitive struggles and being the listening ear during times of trouble. Yet the knife of deception and disappointment lurks around the corner from the very woman whose hand you held just that Sunday, only to hurt you on Monday.

As women leaders we serve more with our heart than our head. This serves as a disadvantage in moving forward because the heart is a deep felt area that pulls at the soul's realm. And we know the soulish realm deals in emotions, wills and feelings.

So when these areas are fragmented it affects our

ability to keep focused on the real enemy which is

not one another, but the enemy.   As a Pastor and life

coach for many women, I have been blessed to lead

many women forward in life. Some I even call my

Spiritual daughters. Yet because I have such a high

expectations of others because of how I push myself

in areas of excellence, it has disappointed me

through the years to see that the same passion I felt

was not in those who I was birthing forth. At times I

would just cry out to the Lord, due to not

understanding why I was being committed and

dedicated to excellence. But I realized that the

people I was crying about were not even dedicated

to their own vision, so I could not expect them to be dedicated to mine.

I am learning more and more to GUARD my heart and allow the Holy Spirit to be my security system!

REFLECTION KEYS TO KEEPING A GUARDED HEART

- During times in which we are challenged it is very critical that we keep a posture of expectation in God, NOT IN humans! We must adjust the lenses of our faith and reflect on the Phenomenal Power of God! He is able to do the supernatural and cause things to shift into alignment in our lives, no matter the situation we are facing.

- You must make a determined decision to discipline your thoughts and conversations.

- You must examine the words you speak and not overlook the importance of keeping your emotions submitted to the will of the Holy Spirit.

- You must remember you have purpose for the Kingdom. Jeremiah 29:11 the Word says, *"For He knows the plan He has for us to prosper and not to fail for an expected end."* The steps of purpose have so many unexpected twist and turns, yet we must walk in Kingdom courage and not allow discouragement to overwhelm us.

The purpose of God involves

disappointments, mistakes and successes.

- The ingredients of what God chooses to use

  to construct our purpose is filled with a

  variety of spices that challenge the taste buds

  of life to awaken to realities that can make or

  break us. The choice is yours on how you

  choose to digest your purpose, not another

  person.

NOW IS THE TIME TO MOVE BEYOND THE ORDINARY

As you take steps forward into activating your phenomenal breakthrough, you must boldly take a Kingdom stand within and stretch your life to reach forth into new horizons of ideas and positive thoughts. As I continue to strive forth in my life, I have had to aggressively take hold of belief in myself and not get stuck in the doorway called "stagnation". When you become stagnant, you fail to dream for better. You begin to get comfortable to a wilderness situation that brings no sense of

expansion in your life. The Word shares, *Behold, I*

have commanded a widow there to provide for you.

So he arose and went to Zarephath. When he came

to the gate of the city, behold, a widow was there

gathering sticks. He called to her, Bring me a little

water in a vessel that I may drink. As she was going

to get it, he called to her and said, bring me a

morsel of bread in your hand. And she said, As the

Lord your God lives, I have not a loaf baked but

only a handful of meal in the jar and a little oil in

the bottle. See, I am gathering two sticks, that I may

go in and bake it for me and my son that we may eat

it--and die. Elijah said to her, Fear not; go and do

as you have said. But make me a little cake of [it]

first and bring it to me, and afterward prepare some

for yourself and your son household ate for many

*days. (*1 King 17: 1-15)

The story of the widow woman in the word of

God is a great example of a woman whose stagnant

perspective of life caused her to expect death as her

only escape. Due to her lack of food and money, she

began to limit her abilities and lost sight of her

purpose in the midst of this temporary situation.

IT IS TIME FOR YOU TO DIG DEEP

1) At this time in your life have you lost sight of

the ability to still dream big? If yes, then what

steps can you take to resurrect your dream,

career or ministry?

_____

_____

_____

_____

_____

_____

_____

2) Your dream is still capable of living, yet you must beware "stagnations." What is holding you back from taking a risk?

_____

_____

_____

_____

_____

_____

_____

3) We fall in the trap of looking for too much
   validation from others. This stronghold lies
   in the matrix of wounds inflicted by others.
   God wants you to get entangled in Him.
   Therefore, whose voice has more authority in
   your life than God? Why?

_____

_____

_____

_____

_____

_____

_____

_____

Daily Applications:

- Gird up with spiritual armor

- Gauge your thinking

- Serve with humility

ACTIVATION FOR PHENOMENAL
BREAKTHROUGHS

Many women are in a critical place of their

destiny. Therefore, you have to guard who you let in

your sphere and what thoughts you give permission

to remain in your thoughts. *Now the mind of the*

flesh [which is sense and reason without the Holy

Spirit] is death [death that [a]comprises all the

miseries arising from sin, both here and hereafter].

But the mind of the [Holy] Spirit is life and [soul]

peace [both now and forever]. [That is] because the

*mind of the flesh [with its carnal thoughts and purposes] is hostile to God, for it does not submit itself to God's Law; indeed it cannot. (*Romans 8:6-7). You have to ask yourself if your thoughts have the capability to push you forward. If not then you must make a decision to change them by applying the Word of God to those death thoughts. Yet because of God's love for us He will cause Divine interruptions to come into our lives in hopes to shift us to another level of faith.

In the Book of 1Kings 17, the widow woman doesn't understand her destiny is being interrupted by the prophet Elijah. A prophet comes to knock at your door to activate, regulate and bring revelation. The mantle of Elijah is on the body of Christ, therefore, get up from your dry place and move in the Elijah anointing.

This anointing caused the widow to be an entrepreneur within 24 hours. Your life will never be the same. The mantle isn't limited to the four walls of the church; it's a supernatural oil that flows on anyone who wants it. You have to know the resume of people's lives before letting them in your life. God steps in your life to blow your mind and those who are watching. Learn to keep God first. What are you sacrificing this season to make room for God? First fruit is a sacrifice to increase. It blows on the rest of the harvest so it won't go dry.

Daily Applications:

- Stand on the Word (or Stand on your word?)

- Be humble

- Place God first in your life

RAISE UP YOUR EXPECTATIONS

Women of God you must expect phenomenal breakthroughs from God. You must activate faith for phenomenal breakthroughs to happen in your life. There are times when spiritual brooks dry up. Sometimes a marriage gets a little dry or your health seems to go. Sometimes your finances dry up. In this season of transition we are being repositioned into our destiny. Most of our jobs are training centers, not remaining centers. Your temporary

place is preparing you for your permanent place.
When Elijah was sent to the brook he was in a place
of transition. (Read 1 Kings God sends you
somewhere small and you want to go somewhere
big. He'll first see how faithful you are in the little
assignments.

To be faithful means to execute excellence
even with the small things. Therefore, you must be
determined to execute excellence with your projects,
ministries, finances, and family no matter what
stage they are in. Let me remind you to be faithful
with something is to complete it, even when storms
arise. You must choose to have eyes of an eagle and
soar above the storm. Therefore, you must refuse to
NOT take mess this season so that nothing can

hinder your BEST!

STEPS TO BEING FAITHFUL IN YOUR SMALL SEASON, AWAITING THE BIG

1) There are seasons of birthing, and each season has its own ingredients, but you have to be able to discern if it's a birthing time or a waiting time.

2) You must believe in your layover seasons that God has not forgotten you. Your layover is your place of preparation for fresh revelation.

3) God will allow you to start small, not because your dream is small, but because God is allowing your inner parts of your mind to be renewed and transformed.

4) The Holy Spirit must see something different in our lives, in order, that He can birth forth a new dimension of greatness!

REFLECTION TIME:

1.) The direction of your thoughts must target faith in your waiting season. God will dry up some things because He has something better. He doesn't want you to get used to the ordinary. There is too much in our lives to be ordinary. What are you doing in your life for something to respond to it?

_____

_____

_____

_____

_____

_____

_____

_____

_____

_____

_____

_____

_____

_____

_____

2) As you walk through this God faith journey the process of your thinking is constantly in need of transformation in the Word of God. It's phenomenal that you even woke this morning. Keep in mind sometimes you may want a breakthrough, but God

has to break you. What does it mean for God to

break you? For example, God may need to break

your need to please people so your focus is more

directed to pleasing Him. What areas has God had

to break you in?

_____

_____

_____

_____

_____

_____

_____

_____

_____

_____

3.) Please remember to not conform to the flesh, submit to God, and remember God dries things up so that you can drive up to Him. Therefore, remember a dry up is a drive up. The Word of God says, *"Pride comes before a fall"*. (Proverbs 16:18) There are times God needs us to hit rock bottom, so that when He promotes you your head (pride) will not get in the way. Humility comes when God knows you can handle bad and dirty situations. Can God trust you with something phenomenal? If so how will you ensure that you keep "pride" from getting you off course?

_____

_____

_____

_____

_____

_____

_____

_____

THE IMPORTANCE OF STARVING THE FLESH TO OBTAIN GOD'S BEST

As I move through my own personal pains of disappointments, I have found that when God allows these things, it is not detrimental. Instead it is God ushering me into new places of intimacy with HIM.

I have found times in ministry in which I was in expectation for certain doors to open and just the opposite would occur. It was during these times that I would have to press past negative thoughts and choose to trust God's direction in my life. One thing I have realized is God will kill some situations to stop them from being your God. One of God's main intentions for our lives is that we draw close to the heartbeat of His love and everything else is secondary in His sight.

REFLECTION TIME

1) Remember God wants to be your everything. He wants to be first priority in your life. What is in your life that could be hindering this type of intimacy with God?

_____

_____

_____

_____

_____

_____

_____

_____

_____

_____

_____

_____

_____

_____

2) As you humble yourself in His presence you must

have a teachable posture, in order, to hear His quiet

still voice speak to your heart. What is the status of

your heart condition and how teachable is it?

_____

_____

_____

_____

_____

_____

_____

_____

_____

_____

3) You must be careful about what you are agreeing with in your heart. How positive are your conversations?

_____

_____

_____

_____

_____

_____

_____

_____

_____

_____

ARE YOU READY FOR SPIRITUAL BATTLE

Too many women of God are in the spiritual
emergency room (E.R.). I understand we are in the
hospital healing spiritual, but I believe we have to
make room for some more people with real
emergencies. We must learn how to erase our past.
If we do not erase it, then it has the ability to
resurrect and harm our spiritual growth. Yet when
we are in warfare for our lives and families we must
stand on the Word of God! *The Word of God says,*

So shall my word be that goes forth out of my mouth: it shall not return to Me void {without producing any effect, useless}, but it shall accomplish that which I please and purpose, and it shall prosper in the thing for which I sent it (Isaiah 55:11 AMP).

Therefore, the Word shall come to pass, it doesn't have a choice. You need to recognize your **real** enemy. The wrestling match is not with one another, women of God, but it's with the enemy. The Word says, *We wrestle not against flesh and blood, but against world rulers of this present darkness....*(Eph 6:12) Therefore, we must continue to exercise our spiritual authority. Authority is not walking around looking like you're somebody important; nor is it pointing your fingers and shaking your head as if you are big and bad. Authority is when you put a demand on the promises of God for your life. It is so clear that if the heart of the flesh is not circumcised, then you get paralyzed in the spirit. You get paralyzed in your condition of loving, giving to others and even in seeing yourself for who you really are. You can't see me for who I am if you can't see yourself for who you are. Oftentimes, we can't stay in a maintenance place because we don't maintain our integrity. We can't even maintain our own love. We should be seeing and getting something new in our lives. We should see new promises and new breakthroughs.

We have to know there has to be something more for us as God's phenomenal women!

Therefore, you must put a demand on your authority in God. In other words, do not allow yourself to be governed by natural authority and try to run above your husband's authority or your Pastor's authority or your supervisor's authority. You must stand in your Kingdom position in the Spirit realm and fight from that posture.

You must break the generational curses of Jezebel, rejection, fear and abandonment (*for more on these spirits purchase my CD teachings*), because something should be breaking of your family by now. You must recognize that it is time for reversals and you must realize some curses should not be repeated. Some situations do not need to continue to manifest, and you must ensure that you are not the avenue that the enemy can use to keep the curse from reverse.

You are God's mighty warrior, but do you know what you are fighting this season? (*Take a moment to meditate*) What spirits have you noticed continue to show themselves in your life and family? And what is your WAR plan to gain victory?

_____

_____

_____

_____

_____

_____

_____

_____

_____

_____

_____

_____

WAR TOOLS TO USE IN BATTLE:

- The Power of the Blood of Jesus! Apply it daily on yourself and family!

- Confess the Word of God daily with Kingdom Authority

- Allow praise to saturate your atmosphere to serve as shield against the devices of the enemy!

- Begin to incorporate FASTING in your life at least once a week or more.

- Take yourself through personal deliverance on a weekly or daily basis.

- Allow the Holy Spirit to show you what spirits are in your blood line so you have clarity on what you are fighting.

- Study and gain knowledge on Spiritual warfare and purchase materials to teach you on the names of Strongholds so you can fight with precision. (For more information on warfare and deliverance please go to my website www.lsrtalks.com) This is your season for VICTORY!

THE WRESTLING MATCH

The wrestling match requires a paradigm shift as you mature in your destiny and begin to desire new opportunities. You must not allow people to label you by your past. Too many times we define who we are by where we come from, instead, of the new DNA of your salvation. In Genesis when God called out Adam and he said he was afraid and hid himself and God said "who told you, you were naked". My question is who told you that you were broke, ugly, and unable to go to college? Many of you have been walking around accepting these types of perspectives and allowed people's limited views to shape the definition of your character and life.

I want to help someone step out the boat of limited thinking into unlimited possibility. I know you have not had success in everything, but this cannot be the finale of your life. We must allow the God's metamorphosis process to take place. God will call out of you what you have not seen before. In other words, you might be in poverty, but God will bring wealth out it. Therefore you say "I am rich in Jesus name! I am moving forward, the best is yet to cone in my life!" Remember God wants to bring something new out of something old. God wants to "shift" your life. I believe God is speaking

to the seed of potential within you right this

moment. Thus, as women of God we have to know

each day God is speaking to dormant seeds of

potential in each of us, and we must not allow the

old nature to stifle us from new expansions of life

and victory in our destiny!

Keys That Can Hinders Your Paradigm Shift

1) We must review the people who we have allowed

to have a voice in our lives. Therefore, you must

ensure you surround yourself with people who are

ready to "Shift" with you!

2) You must not press REWIND on the tape

recorder of your mind you must press FORWARD.

3) You must say though I am weak, "I AM Strong",

I might be poor, but I AM RICH! You have to speak words of FAITH even in the midst of the battle within!

4) Remember when God shifts your potential everything connected to your life because things you thought could not move or would not move will MOVE! Everything that can be shaken will be. Therefore, do not get upset when people leave. It is a part of the Phenomenal Shift taken place in life!

Daily Applications:

- I know I'm in a wrestling match and I will be wrestling until Jesus comes. Yet, this I do know is I will come out VICTORIOUS!

- Acknowledge your real enemy is not people but the devil!

- Exercise spiritual authority.

- Let go of the past and move toward your

  future.

HOW TO DEAL WITH SEEMINGLY DEAD SITUATIONS

*Now Jesus loved Martha and her sister and Lazarus. [They were His dear friends, and He held them in loving esteem'] Therefore [even] when He heard that Lazarus was sick, He still stayed two days longer in the same place where He was (*John 11:5-6).

These are two women dealing with a situation that appeared dead. In this situation Jesus heard about your condition, but He still waited. You must understand that Jesus wants to know if your condition remains the same will you keep pushing for a breakthrough. Now take note of the level of faith Martha had. *Martha then said to Jesus, Master if You had been here, my brother would not have died.* (John 11: 21) Jesus didn't come, yet their brother was dead. Have you been in a situation that seemed dead or had a problem where there seemed to be no solution? If this is you, then you must walk in the confidence and then speak the Word and believe the Word that says, "*And even now I know that whatever you ask from God, He will grant it to you. And even now I know that whatever you ask from God, He will grant it to you.*"(John 11:22).

As you step into deeper levels of intimacy

with God, you can have a moment of doubt.   But,

after you have that moment you need to recognize

the power of God. God can change any situation.

Don't let your moment be a lifetime. There is

something in you God is still trying to restore.

Beloved, I pray that you may prosper in every way

and [that your body] may keep well, even as [I

know] your soul keeps well and prospers. (3 John

1:2) Sometimes it may be that something in you

isn't rich enough to receive blessings from God,

therefore, be careful of what you allow to reside in

your thoughts. You must be determined to see

results in your life.

The Word says, *Jesus said to her, **I AM***

[Myself] the Resurrection and the Life, Whoever

*believes in (adheres to, trusts in, and relies on) Me, although he may die, yet he shall live (*John 11:25). I know what you know but I AM. The key is whoever **believes.** You need to really, really believe that God is doing something in your life. Then the I AM comes up. How do you know when I AM has come? When you have everything you need. Everything you need comes with I AM. If I AM is in my life, I'm not sick or broke because he loves me too much to leave me without. If I am still lacking then, I haven't encountered I AM.

There's a push on the women of God concerning the posture of our mouth. Always remember your mouth can create greatness or diffuse it. Therefore, get your mind off of self; it prevents the I Am from coming. It's not about you; it's about touching lives, delivering souls, and setting the captive free and healings. Ask God this question. What is missing from me that keeps me from experiencing I AM?

The Word of God says, *When the Jews who were sitting with her in the house and consoling her saw how hastily Mary had risen and gone out, they followed her, supposing that she was going to the tomb to pour out her grief there.* (John 11:31) Women of God remember Jesus does not cause things to come to hurt your feelings, but to change your paradigm. You may be in the emergency room, but He doesn't want you there for the same thing. After awhile you get immune to certain things. Your test is bringing reformation. You better learn God in your trial.

Martha dropped down to the feet of Jesus. . If you question God, question with humility. Don't forget who He is. He is the King of Kings the Lord of Lords. You cannot get haughty with Him. Haughtiness has you thinking you deserve something; it's only the righteousness of God that qualifies you. There is a dichotomy, a key difference, between boldness and haughtiness. Humility is boldly reminding Him about promises with humility in our heart, while standing on His Word. She humbled herself at His feet. Keep yourself in a posture of worship. God is going to open our minds to receive truth and revelation.

The power of the mind can bring supernatural

breakthroughs.

REFLECTION TIME: WAYS TO STEP INTO

NEW ADVANCEMENTS OF YOUR LIFE

1) Ask yourself " Why am I afraid to trust God?"

Now write steps you can take to trust God more in

this season of your life.

_____

_____

_____

_____

_____

_____

_____

_____

_____

_____

_____

_____

_____

_____

2) You must challenge yourself to see change despite how things may seem in the natural. You must have a determination to get your life together because some holdups are because we are holding back. Remove the stones in your life by using your Kingdom faith and worship! List stones in your life that you will not allow to remain in your perception

on life:

_____

_____

_____

_____

_____

_____

_____

_____

_____

_____

_____

_____

3) This is a season in which your emotions cannot be in the driver's seat. You must remain focused on God's Word and use it as a standard for how you respond to situations. How can you maintain the right attitude in the face of negative stresses?

_____

_____

_____

_____

_____

_____

_____

_____

_____

KEYS TO TAPPING INTO UNLIMITED FAITH

As women of God, remember when believing

for Phenomenal Breakthroughs opposition is an

open door for opportunity. God knows the work that

He's started in your life, every detail from Genesis

to Revelation. You must have the confidence to

know that God will see you through! Hebrews 11:1

(NKJ) *"Now faith is the substance of things hoped*

for, the evidence of things not seen". Therefore, you

must learn how to build your confidence. When God

has predestined you for a thing, it will manifest, no matter what others say or think regarding that matter.

God specializes in doing the impossible even in the midst of a dramatic situation! The Word shares a storyline concerning David. *So David and his men came to the city, and there it was, burned with fire, and their wives, their sons, and their daughters had been taken captive. (*1 Samuel 30:3 NKJ) Please keep in mind David was a man after God's own heart, and he still had drama in his life. Believers have to go through trials and tribulations just like unbelievers. *Now David was greatly distressed, for the people spoke of stoning him, because the soul of all the people was grieved, every man for his sons* *and his daughters. But David strengthened himself*

*in the Lord his God (*1 Samuel 30:6 NKJ).

As you read the Word above, you must

remember although you can't trace God, it doesn't

mean that He's left your side. Thus, it is important

that you do not allow stress, fear, and worry to

causes you to reach out (instead of reaching up) to

things that have no solutions. Notice in the Word of

God, David chose to seek the face of God in his

situation. The Word of God says, *So David inquired*

of the Lord, saying, "Shall I pursue this troop? Shall

I overtake them?" And He answered him, "Pursue,

for you shall surely overtake them and without fail

*recover all (*1 Samuel 30:8). You must realize that

when you are in your distressed place, be careful

who you seek advice from. Continue to know in your situation you do not need reasoning, you need revelation. When God is after something inside of you, He stretches you more than you've ever stretched before. In the midst of the stretch you will find yourself dealing with targets of lack of confidence which produces nuggets of weariness. Thus, you must reflect on the times God extended His love and mercy and allow the antibiotics of God's truth to cause healing and STRENGTH within. This is not your season to give up! You must do like David did and encourage yourself in the Lord on a daily basis. I decree you will be triumphant in the face of the enemy.

APPLY THESE KEYS FOR 7 DAYS AND SHARE

WITH DR. RICH YOUR EXPERIENCES AT

INFO@LSRTALKS.COM

Keys to Tapping into Your Unlimited Faith

1. Jesus wants you healed – recognize it!

Mark 2:17 reads: Jesus overhearing, shot back,

"Who needs a doctor: the healthy or the sick? I'm

here inviting the sin-sick, not the spiritually-fit."

2. Hold fast to your confession.

Hebrews 4:14-15 reads: Now that we know what we

have – Jesus, this great High Priest with ready

access to God – let's not let it slip through our

fingers. We don't have a priest who is out of touch

with our reality. He's been through weakness and

testing, experienced it all – all but the sin.

NOTE: Your confession is your faith in Him (Jesus Christ).

3. You must come out of your condemnation and confess.

Psalm 62:5 reads: God, the One and Only – I'll wait as long as He says. Everything I hope for comes from Him, so why not?

4. Have courage to face your pain.

Job 1:20 reads: Job got to his feet, ripped his robe, shaved his head, then fell to the ground and worshiped.

5. Forgive and let go.

Colossians 3:2 reads: Set your mind on things above, not on things on the earth.

NOTE: How dare you empower your enemy by being angry?

Colossians 3:12-13 reads: So, chosen by God for this new life of love, dress in the wardrobe God picked out for you: compassion, kindness, humility, quiet strength, discipline. Be even-tempered; contend with second place, quick to forgive an offense. Forgive as quickly and completely as the Master forgave you.

6. God will send a lifeline to you (male or female).

James 5:16 reads: Make this your common practice: Confess your sins to each other and pray for each other so that you can live together whole and healed. The prayer of a person living right with God is something powerful to be reckoned with.

7. Find comfort in God's Word.

Psalm 119:50 reads: These Words hold me up in bad

times: yes, your promises rejuvenate me.

8. Confess the areas where you have sinned.

9. Engage in spiritual warfare.

Ephesians 6:10 reads: And that about wraps it up.

God is strong, and He *wants you strong. So take*

everything the Master has set out for you, well made

weapons of the best materials!

WHAT IS THE ROOT OF OUR ACTIONS

We must realize that issues in our lives stem

from within. This is why react the way we do.

Whether you are dealing with rejection,

unforgiveness, abandonment or fear these areas

cause us to put walls up that hinder you from letting

others in. This action extends itself toward our

relationship with God. These heart issues affect us

in producing healthy relationships. Therefore, we

must take bold steps to come real with God and

ourselves. The Word says it is the place from which the issues of our lives originate (Proverbs 4:23). The origins of our issues are not too deep for God to reach. For this to happen, you must allow God's love intimate time in His presence in worship and prayer. These keys are necessary, in order, for inner healing to truly occur within and remain!

REFLECTION TIME: EXAMINE YOUR PRAYER LIFE

1) What is a description of your prayer life?

_____

_____

_____

_____

_____

_____

_____

_____

2) You must not allow conflict to rule you; instead, you must be ready to talk with God. You must remember He is always open to listen to you. You must talk to God like a friend and expect to receive insight. Reflect on a difficult time in your life. How did you communicate with God?

_____

_____

_____

_____

_____

_____

_____

_____

_____

_____

_____

_____

3) You must trust God's ability to help you and to

heal you. God's love is unending. However, we

must choose to accept self-acceptance and self-love

for ourselves. What is hindering you from accepting

yourself?

_____

_____

_____

_____

_____

_____

_____

_____

_____

_____

_____

_____

_____

_____

4) What steps are you willing to take to adjust your

inner perspective concerning self?

_____

_____

_____

_____

_____

_____

_____

_____

_____

_____

_____

_____

_____

_____

_____

Decree this prayer : I have Kingdom Authority and this gives me the right to use the name "Jesus." My authority is sealed in the Blood of Jesus. I am yielding to the Holy Spirit inwardly and new healing is birthing forth within! *You therefore must endure hardship as a good soldier of Jesus Christ.* (2 Timothy 2:3 NKJ). I decree I am God's good soldier and I shall walk forth with NEW VICTORY because this is my time to RISE FORTH!!! I decree *I have pursued my enemies and overtaken them; neither did I turn back again till they were destroyed* (Psalm 18:37 NKJ). In Jesus Name amen!

Daily Applications:

- You must take on the anointing of preservation to keep walking in victory just as David did.

- You must remind yourself daily that opposition is an opportunity for God to move on your behalf. Your emotions describe your situation, not who you are! Therefore, YOU WILL RECOVER ALL!

- Build your confidence through God

- Seek wise counsel

- Walk in Kingdom authority

NEVER GIVE UP!

As women of God we are to NEVER give up on our dreams or aspirations. We must not allow the enemy to tackle our faith with arrows of hopelessness. We must allow God's boldness to arise within and stand strong in His promises The Words says, *And let us not lose heart and grow weary and faint in acting nobly and doing right, for in due time and at the appointed season we shall reap, if we do not loosen or relax our courage and faint* (Galatians 6:9 AMP).

We must stand in the faith and trust that God is in full control of our destiny and He will not allow our lives to be defeated! As daughters of the Most High God, we are to never give up! The Word says,

The Lord does not delay and is not tardy or slow about what He promises, according to some people's conception of slowness, but He is long-suffering (extraordinarily patient) toward you, not desiring that any should perish, but that all should turn to repentance (2 Peter 3:9 AMP). God is long-suffering towards us, therefore, do not judge your conditions by what you see in the natural. God is not slack, He is faithful! To be slack means to be negligent; careless; weak; and tense. God is faithful to His Word!

As long as you speak the Word of God – He has to be faithful. Again, God is not slack in His promises. God is constantly moving internally and externally in our lives.

Decree these words daily: It is done! You will not take some of your present burdens into the next year, because your season of favor is upon you. Begin to rise up in the confidence of the Lord. Due season and appointed time go hand in hand!!! *For I know the thoughts and plans that I have for you, says the Lord, thoughts and plans for welfare and peace and not for evil, to give you hope in your final outcome (*Jeremiah29:11).

Your Present Condition Is Not Your Permanent Condition!

This is the season that you must be determined that present conditions in your life are changing despite the arrows the enemy may send to detour or even devour your faith. The Word says, *THE WEAPONS MAY FORM BUT THEY SHALL NOT PROSPER* (Isaiah 54:17). The redeeming power of God is your safety net this season! You must grab hold of the NOW Victory within your

Spirit and make a decision to walk forth and not allow the voice of the enemy to detour your decision. You have overcome many struggles and your life is closer to new dimensions of healing and restoration despite what you feel within. Therefore, on this day you must put on your bulletproof vest by offering a continual sacrifice of praise. *Hebrews 13:15 says "...let us offer the sacrifice of praise to God, that is, the fruit of our lips, giving thanks to His name."* You must defy the odds of your circumstances and begin to recognize the strength of your praise and deny the influence of the flesh that wants to complain and murmur about your present condition.

APPLICATION KEYS OF AN OVERCOMER:

- Remember you are an "Overcomer," therefore you are no longer a victim. You are victorious and you will not lose sight of the greatness that awaits your arrival.

- Remember the enemy can only form the missile, but you can deactivate it with your PRAISE!

- Your praise HAS penetrating power through the blood of Jesus, so open your mouth and make the devil recognize you still are ARMED AND DANGEROUS!

- You walk in the Redeeming POWER of the Blood of Jesus! SHOUT GLORY

AIM FOR VICTORY

This is your season of "**Victory**" as God's believer! The key element is staying FREE from "**Entanglement!**" The word "**entanglement**" means to be hindered from progressing forward. The Word of God says, *In this freedom Christ has made us free; stand fast then, and do not be hampered and held ensnare and submit again to a yoke of slavery (which you have once put off)* (Gal. 5:25 AMP).

Therefore, the operation tactics of

entanglement is to construct a web effect that will

cause the believer to get frustrated and want to give

up. This is why we must trust in the "**Greater One**"

who is Christ our Lord and Savior to breathe new

life within our Spirit man daily.

I decree in Jesus' name as a Prophet of

God: this is your season to walk in Great

VICTORY!! And there is a stirring forth of

determination despite the arrows of the enemy

arising in your Spirit. So continue to know that there

is a Prophetic Wind reversing the schemes of the

enemy and as God's phenomenal woman you are

making a "**Decision**" to stay FREE!! In the NAME

OF JESUS!!

Daily Applications:

- Stay focused on the winning prize.

- Write your vision on a paper or poster and put it on your wall.

- Believe God like you never have before!

ON THE VERGE OF A BREAKTHROUGH

At about four o'clock in the morning, Jesus came toward them walking on the water. They were scared out of their wits. "A ghost!" they said, crying out in terror. But Jesus was quick to comfort them. "Courage, it's Me. Don't be afraid." Peter, suddenly bold, said, "Master, if it's really You, call me to come to you on the water." He said, "Come ahead." Jumping out of the boat, Peter walked on the water to Jesus. But when he looked down at the waves

churning beneath his feet, he lost his nerve and started to sink. He cried, "Master, save me!" Jesus didn't hesitate. He reached down and grabbed his hand. Then He said, "Faint – heart, what got into you?" (Matthew 14:26-36 The Message Bible).

As you can see from the text above, turbulence produces a crisis that will position you for the next level. Like Peter, you must be willing to take a risk with your faith. You will always be faced with the choice to remain stagnated. Faith is the insurance that keeps you walking in the Kingdom Principle. Begin to move with more acceleration this season and apply ***Focus Faith!*** To apply focus faith you must set some goals and aim to reach them with a deepened level of determination. You must not allow doubt or fear to hinder your progress!

This is your season to progress forward and experience manifestations on the earth realm.

YOU MUST PURSUE FORWARD AND APPLY THESE KEYS:

1) Remember stillness comes because of your fear of getting no results. You must activate faith despite how things look in the natural.

2) Don't put limits on your faith. Take the limits off and trust God for the impossible!

3) You are applying faith on a daily basis by decreeing the Word of God on a daily basis and expecting results!

Decree these words in prayer: I am on the

verge of a breakthrough and wide and effective

doors are opening for my destiny! I have favor

on my life; therefore, I will walk in faith and not

in fear in Jesus name. I am empowered to obtain

Victory through the power of the Blood of the

Lamb!

KEYS TO OPENING THE DOOR OF BLESSINGS

I must stress to you the importance of reminding yourself on a daily basis that *God knows the plans He has for you, plans to prosper and not to fail for an expected end* (Jeremiah 29:11). This can only be done through the renewing of your mind. This renewal of your mind is done through the power of the Holy Spirit and it requires a shift in your perspective. You can't keep the same paradigm of thinking. As I continue to grow in being a better servant, leader, mom and wife I have embraced the

importance of not allowing past thoughts to stifle

my trust in God. I have endured many trials in

ministry and life, yet I have learned to not allow the

disappointments of my journey to blur my vision of

believing for something better!

See the important thing about staying in the

driving lane of better is that it helps you to avoid

becoming BITTER. The bite of bitterness can cause

trouble that births unforgiveness. This

unforgiveness can paralyze the effectiveness of your

keys of authority in the Heavenly Life. Thus, you

must "guard" your heart and not allow the issues of

life to terminate your breakthrough in prayer!

In the Word of God, Martha and Mary were

challenged to apply a paradigm shift in their

thinking and apply FOCUS FAITH concerning

Lazarus despite the situation. The Word of God

shares, "*NOW A certain man named Lazarus was ill.*

He was of Bethany, the village where Mary and her

sister Martha lived. This Mary was the one who

anointed the Lord with perfume and wiped His feet

with her hair. It was her brother Lazarus who was

[now] sick...... So then Jesus told them plainly,

Lazarus is dead, And for your sake I am glad that I

was not there; it will help you to believe (to trust

and rely on Me). However, let us go to him. Then

Thomas, who was called the Twin, said to his fellow

disciples, Let us go too, that we may die [be killed]

along with Him. So when Jesus arrived, He found

that he [Lazarus] had already been in the tomb four

days. Bethany was near Jerusalem, only about two

miles away, and a considerable number of the Jews

had gone out to see Martha and Mary to console

them concerning their brother. When Martha heard

that Jesus was coming, she went to meet Him, while

Mary remained sitting in the house. Martha then

said to Jesus, Master, if You had been here, my

brother would not have died. And even now I know

that whatever You ask from God, He will grant it to

You. Jesus said to her, your brother shall rise again.

Martha replied, I know that he will rise again in the

resurrection at the last day. Jesus said to her, I am

[Myself] the Resurrection and the Life. Whoever

believes in (adheres to, trusts in, and relies on) Me,

although he may die, yet he shall live; (John 11:1-25

AMP)

As you read the text above you can see that Mary and Martha were in a seemingly dead situation. You may be wrestling with a seemingly dead situation and ask yourself, "Why am I not seeing the open doors?" Although you may ask this question, don't let the questioning last a lifetime. You must know that too many questions may limit your ability to hear clearly from God. When God doesn't give the answer, just trust that He will reveal it in another way. Some things look like they can't happen, but God said we are in a place where some things can resurrect. As long as there is a seed of faith, there is the ability for God to step in. Woman of God remember God likes things to seem impossible so He can bring it to pass for His Glory. God is still the Great I AM, the King of Kings and the Lord of Lords!

REFLECTION TIME: YOUR TIME OF TESTING

1) God is speaking to someone's situation that may look dead. Where are your emotions this season? Have you chosen to have focused faith despite what your emotions are saying? If so, in what way?

_____

_____

_____

_____

_____

_____

_____

_____

_____

_____

_____

2) List some people or situations you need to

release from your heart. Now, list some positive

things or people that have occurred in your life.

_____

_____

_____

_____

_____

_____

_____

_____

_____

_____

_____

3) Define how you will apply FOCUS FAITH in the areas of your job, family or finances:

_____

_____

_____

_____

_____

_____

Decree these words now: I am looking forward to

the supernatural. I am going beyond my normal

portion! Yes someone just walked into a new door

of Breakthrough! I AM NO LONGER afraid to

believe for God's Best in my life! I will not allow

the enemy or unbelief to hinder this next place of

victory that is birthing forth upon my life in Jesus

name!

CONCLUSION AND REFLECTION TIME

Your life is taken hold of new chapter.

Woman of God old things have passed away and all

things are coming into the New. You have embraced

a new identity of who you are and how you should

live in the promises of God, in a place of hope no

matter what!

After all, you are the righteousness of Jesus

Christ; therefore, you have a right to receive His

benefits. As a joint heir with Christ Jesus, you are

seated in heavenly places. As a phenomenal woman

of God you must execute the Law of repetition which are daily confessions repeating who you are and whose you are. You must make the decision to imagine yourself as a great person, wealthy and healed. You must continue to see by faith new doors opening for your life, see your body healed, and see Divine connections taking place in your life.

As you continue to turn the pages of your destiny forward, see your kids walking in favor, your husband as the priest and prophet of your home, see your finances multiplying and be determined that the BEST is still yet to come in your life and all those connected to your life! Woman of God you have taken hold of a NEW PERSPECTIVE! I can sense in the Spirit realm your insight has shifted upward and you will no longer be held in captivity

to the past. I bless God for the honor that you and I

connected as SISTERS in Christ! I pray the

Kingdom connection remains. Please keep me

updated on the new exploits and goals you and the

Holy Spirit obtain!! Let's stay connected!! By the

way what is your name?

PHENOMENAL WOMAN,

nice to meet you.

That's my name too!

_____

PERSONAL NOTE FROM DR. RICH:

If you catch the revelation of God's love for you and how much He truly wants you walking in new doors of Victory your life will supernaturally birth forth a phenomenal breakthrough! This in turn, will cause doubt to be cut at the root of those old conditions and cause new repositions in your life. God wants to speak to the root of some of your situations so you won't keep seeing the same results. I hear the Lord speaking to someone reading this book now and saying, "He wants you to have more than enough, and exceed your expectations. After all, you are God's Phenomenal Woman!"

As God's phenomenal woman you may need some

extra encouragement or need someone to coach you

through the steps of your success. If so please

contact Dr. Rich at info@lsrtalks.com. Also if you

would like to use this book as a handbook for your

ministry or book, please contact us at

info@lsrtalks.com.

12006925R00074

Made in the USA
Charleston, SC
04 April 2012